"And
After That
The
Judgement"

by

Natalie
Vellacott

Copyright

Chapter 1

Annie realises that she is lying face down on the ground. As she takes a quick glance around, all she can see is a dazzlingly bright light. There is something dreadful and brilliant about the light that makes Annie afraid to look directly at it.

Where is she? The last thing she can remember is that she had been lying in a hospital bed. That's right, it was a routine operation to remove a cyst. Her family had come to visit her before she had been put to sleep.

Am I still being operated on? Is this what it's meant to be like? Annie isn't sure and she feels uneasy.

A loud voice sounds, "Rise up Annie Yale. We have business to do."

Annie puts her hands over her ears. She can't stand the awesomeness of the voice. It's almost painful. *Just a strange dream probably caused by the hospital drugs. Nothing to worry about. I wish it would end, though. It's pretty realistic.*

"It's not a dream Annie, something went wrong during the operation." The voice again, pure, perfect and awesome.

"How can that be? I'm still young and have a lot of time left. It was a routine operation. That's what they said." Annie starts to panic as she realises what the voice is telling her.

I'm dead?!

She plucks up the courage to lift her head and look at the figure standing in front of her. All she can see is the light and the outline of a man.

"You know Who I am, don't you Annie?" The man speaks to her, His voice is stern but there is a hint of sadness.

"You are Jesus." The clarity hits Annie. She knows exactly Who this man is.

"You're wondering how you recognise Me," Jesus says. The sadness is unmistakeable this time. "I've always been there but you never trusted Me."

Annie now recalls falling to the ground and being dazzled by the bright light on arrival. "Where is that light coming from? It's almost blinding."

Jesus shakes His head sadly, "Oh Annie, I know the light is making you a little uncomfortable, but I'm afraid that's the least of your problems."

"What? What do you mean?" Annie is shaken by His words. They have the ring of truth. She is afraid. "Is this heaven?"

"What do you think?" Jesus asks as He gazes at her sorrowfully.

"It doesn't seem like it as I didn't think I would feel afraid in heaven." Annie hadn't realised that she even believed in a place called heaven until now.

"This isn't heaven. It's Judgement Day. You are standing before My throne and we're about to look at your life in detail," Jesus explains.

"What will happen at the end?" Annie whispers. She's almost afraid to ask the question.

"Everything depends on whether the things you did wrong on earth have been dealt with," Jesus is patient.

Annie thinks of the good things she has done in comparison with the bad.

"No, not like that," Jesus clarifies.

"How do you know what I'm thinking?" Annie feels exposed. She doesn't like it.

"Everything is about to be revealed," Jesus says.

Annie now finds herself sitting on a small chair. Two brightly coloured beings are either side of her. She guesses they must be angels. Glancing to her side, she can see the big throne with the brilliant light and the man called Jesus, that she'd immediately recognised.

A big screen is in front of them.

A movie? Annie is still thinking about Jesus' words but she doesn't really understand what is happening.

The screen flashes as images appear. Annie is horrified as she reads the title: *"The life of Annie Yale (1971-2017)". We aren't seriously going to watch a movie of my whole life? I wonder how much detail there will be.*

She doesn't have to wonder about this for long as the first scene begins with clips of Annie as a baby. She is gurgling, laughing and throwing food around. Annie smiles. *Well, at least this part is good.* The thought has only just left her mind when the images change. Annie is now a toddler. She's screaming and shouting at her parents. Then, deliberately tearing a book to pieces and thumping her younger brother David. Annie turns her head away in shame and embarrassment. Then, she thinks better of it. *I was just a small child. We all do things wrong at that age.* She reassures herself.

Jesus and the angels are silent as the movie continues.

Annie feels uncomfortable and has the sudden urge to speak, "Where did you get this footage from?" Even as she says it, she realises the foolish nature of her question.

"I am everywhere and see everything," Jesus answers.

One of the angels pauses the movie.

Are we really going to sit here and watch the whole of my life? Annie wonders.

"Yes, Annie." Jesus is still patient. Annie knows that this is His nature.

"Can't we just skip to the end so that I know what will happen to me?" Annie feels desperate. She has a horrible feeling about the whole situation.

"Annie," Jesus says sadly, "you've never trusted Me with your life or had your sin forgiven. You can't enter heaven."

"So what are we doing this for? Isn't it pointless?" Annie asks although she has a feeling that nothing that is done in this place is ever pointless.

"We are reviewing your life so that you can see why you can't go to heaven and so that you can also see that your punishment is fair," Jesus tells her.

"Punishment? What punishment? How long will it last?" Annie still doesn't understand.

"Oh Annie, it's forever. You rejected the only way for your sins to be forgiven whilst you were on earth." A tear appears in Jesus' eye as He explains.

"Forever? But surely there's something I can do?" Annie starts to cry, softly at first. She wants to believe that this Man is lying but deep down she knows that He cannot lie. *Perhaps I can reason with Him.* "I didn't reject God on earth, well not completely," she submits.

"Let's look at the evidence, shall we?" Jesus replies in a way that causes Annie to fall silent once more.

They turn back to the movie.

Annie is now about four and is trotting into a Sunday school class. She sits and listens as the elderly lady tells the story of *Jonah and the Big Fish* to a group of about ten children.

"See, look, I did learn about God. I didn't reject Him." Annie stops crying, temporarily feeling vindicated by the discovery. She'd forgotten that she went to Sunday school all those years ago. *Phew, that was close. Now I know why my mum forced me to go. Thanks, Mum!*

There is no response from those watching the movie with her. They don't seem to be impressed by her Sunday school attendance. As they continue watching, a bubble appears above Annie's head on the screen. In it is written, "I wonder which dolly mummy will buy me. I like the pink Barbie one best. Oh, this is really boring. I hope it will finish soon."

Annie flushes red. She wants to run to the screen and flick off the monitor. *Surely, they can't be planning to watch all of my thoughts as well as my actions? I don't even remember playing with Barbies. Maybe it's just a guess based on what other children were doing at the time. It can't be my real thoughts, can it?*

"It's much more accurate than that Annie. I told you, I see everything." Jesus tells her whilst keeping focused on the movie.

Annie hangs her head in shame and dreads what's coming next.

Annie sees images of herself at about seven. She is dashing around with other children at a park. Her mum is standing nearby with adults she vaguely recognises as some of the parents of her school friends.

"So, Annie got tired of Sunday school in the end?" one of the ladies asks her mother.

"Yes, I don't think she was really into it anyway. I only sent her as it seemed like the right thing to do, and it gave me a chance to get some house stuff done," Annie's mum replies.

"It's a nice story for kids, but then they reach a certain age." Another lady has joined the conversation.

"At least you tried it. Got to be open-minded and let them look into all the religions." A fourth voice is heard.

The angels look dismayed. "Shall we move this forward?" they address Jesus.

"Yes, but first. I just want Annie to see a little of her friend Jessica," Jesus says. "You remember Jessica, don't you Annie?"

"Sort of, she was one of the other kids from church and we also went to school together. I don't remember seeing her much after the first few years at school, though." Now, Annie is curious.

"No, she took a very different path to you." One of the angels speaks to Annie for the first time.

Jesus looks at the angel. "Let her see for herself. That's the best way."

A small girl with dark hair and plaits appears on the screen. She is kneeling by her bed and it looks like she is praying. "Dear God, please forgive my sin. I know you will because Jesus died for me and made me clean. Help me to do what's right. Also, please get Annie to come back to Sunday school and to be my friend again. Amen." The little girl gets up and into bed where she picks up a book and starts reading.

Annie is astounded. "She prayed for me. Why? I don't even really remember her."

"She prayed for you a lot for a few years. You moved away from her as you found new friends. Jessica's name is in here." The angel speaking pats a huge book on a table that Annie hadn't even noticed until now.

She looks at the cover, *The Book of Life.* "What is that?"

"It's where the names of all those who have trusted Me for forgiveness of their sin are recorded." Jesus has been listening to the conversation and now He speaks.

"So, what happens to people whose names aren't there?" Annie asks. She knows her name won't be there but she keeps hoping there is a way out of the mess she is in.

"We spoke about this before Annie, their sin must be dealt with. Let's watch some more of the film," Jesus instructs.

Jessica wanted to be a good friend and cared about me. I wish I'd paid more attention. Things could've been so different. Annie realises that even at a young age she had been given a friend who could have helped her onto the right path.

Annie cringes as the film has now moved on to her late teenage years. *This is where the bad stuff will really come out. It seems so much worse when I'm not with my friends. It was funny when we were all together.*

The movie skips through drunken nights out and a number of

sexual relationships, the details of which aren't shown on the screen. Annie covers her face with her hands and the angels look away.

Suddenly, the camera zooms in, Annie can be seen walking with two girls.

"I'm Agnostic," Annie tells them.

"Really what is that?" one of the girls asks.

"It means I'm not sure if God is there or not. I guess I'll find out when I die."

There is a stunned silence in the Throne Room as those present absorb her words. "I didn't mean that, I didn't realise." Annie weeps at the realisation that her flippancy and pride seem to have cost her her soul.

"Don't you think that's a bit risky?" Annie's head snaps up as her friend replies. *Is that Helen? I don't even remember this conversation.*

"Why? It's not like I'm an Atheist. I'm leaving room for God to prove Himself, but so far He hasn't." Annie challenges her friend in a mocking tone.

Annie cringes once more and wishes herself far away..

"Isn't the Bible proof enough?" Helen responds. "Really, Annie, I still think it's risky. We're talking about life and death after all. Have you seriously looked into it? Don't you think it's worth just a little of your time?"

How on earth did I respond to that? Annie wonders, but she knows it won't be good.

"Since when have you been part of the Bible-bashing brigade? Life and death, huh! I prefer to live for now. I'll think about that later, like when I'm ninety!" Annie looks triumphantly at her friend.

Helen doesn't even look slightly angry, just terribly sad. She opens her mouth to say something but closes it again. A bubble appears above her head. *This is turning into a pointless discussion that won't be helpful for Annie. I'd better stop. Oh Lord, please open her eyes to the truth, before it's too late. Forgive her foolishness and careless words.*

Now, Annie recognises the expression on Helen's face, she can see the same thing in the eyes of Jesus and the angels, pity mingled with compassion.

The angels have lifted up their wings and covered their faces to shield themselves from the harsh words coming from the screen.

The scene shifts. Helen is alone in a bedroom. There are pieces of coloured paper on the walls. The camera zooms in and Annie can see lists of names. One of the lists is headed "salvation." Annie sees her name, it is number three on the list. The movie shows Helen praying on her bed, then she is praying in church, then a meeting with a group of people, then in her bedroom again. The various clips continue for a long time.

Is the video stuck? Annie again forgets that her thoughts are basically audible.

"No, Annie. Helen prayed for you every day for years even after you lost touch. She also had all her church group praying for you," one of the angels explains.

"Why were they praying for me?" Annie still doesn't get it.

"They were praying for your eyes to be opened to the Truth," the angel explains.

Hmm, it doesn't seem like the prayers worked. Annie wishes there was a way to stop herself thinking or at least to shield her thoughts from Jesus and the angels.

"God heard the many prayers of your friends. He prompted you to listen, but you ignored Him and put it off for later. Your heart became a little harder every time. We don't force anyone to believe, you have a choice," Jesus tells her.

"I don't remember being "prompted," as you call it. Are you sure it was me and not just someone who looks like me?" Annie knows her suggestion is ridiculous. She is sure that Jesus knows everything about her, and that mistakes in this place would be impossible.

"Well, let's see, shall we?" Jesus replies as the video moves on.

Annie watches herself walking alone through a park. She still looks to be in her late teens. In fact, she is wearing the same clothes she was wearing when walking with her friends before. She is listening to some music and humming cheerfully. She stops and sits on a bench. She reaches into a bag and takes out a sandwich.

I do remember eating my lunch in that park quite a lot. It was always very peaceful. I wonder why they are showing me this, it doesn't seem relevant.

Annie eats her sandwich, then closes her eyes apparently enjoying the late afternoon sun on her face. A breeze is blowing and gently lifts up some leaves. It carries them towards Annie. The leaves land near to her feet. Annie opens her eyes as she feels the leaves brush against her leg. She looks down and notices a small screwed up piece of paper in the middle of the leaves. Curious, she picks it up and opens it.

Watching her younger self on the screen, Annie can see the picture of a fence across the front of the piece of paper and the words, "Are you sitting on the fence?" She holds her breath as she waits to see what she did with this paper.

Annie opens the paper, which turns out to be a leaflet, and she is reading it. She looks worried, then irritated, but she keeps on reading. Then, she looks around suspiciously.

There is no one there. She tears up the leaflet and puts it into a bin nearby. She shakes her head as she walks away.

Watching her own hostile reaction, and swift disposal of the seemingly innocuous paper, Annie is confused. "What was that paper? Why did I react like that?"

"It was a Christian leaflet explaining why failing to make a decision about God is the same as rejecting Him," Jesus says. "You sat on the fence for too long Annie and that leaflet was a warning."

"But it was just some rubbish that was blowing around in the wind and happened to land near me. What if I hadn't even picked it up?" Annie can't understand how her response to reading this leaflet can add to her catalogue of woes.

"It wasn't random at all, watch," Jesus replies.

He looks at one of the angels who nods. The video is rewound slightly. A room appears on the screen, a small group of three ladies and three men have their heads bowed as they sit in a circle.

More praying. Great. Annie is beginning to see how things work around here.

"Prayer makes things happen." The angel responds to Annie as if she has spoken aloud.

The small group finish praying, then head out of the building which, from the outside, looks like a church. They are carrying leaflets in their hands. They break away from each other as they head along the street. Annie thinks she can see the front of the leaflet that she had torn up in the hand of one of the group. They start offering the leaflets to people as they pass by. Many refuse to take them but others accept and stuff them into pockets. Some are seen putting them in nearby bins after checking that no one is watching. Annie is relieved that she isn't the only one to have done this.

A man takes a leaflet from one of the church group and continues along the road. Annie recognises the road as the one that leads towards the park. The man is reading the leaflet as he walks but then he grunts, screws it up and throws it into a hedgerow as he walks past the edge of the park.

The video is paused. "Now, do you see, Annie? It wasn't random at all."

Annie shakes her head. She doesn't see. It still seems like pure chance to her.

"I think she needs to see, and hear, the prayer meeting at the beginning," Jesus tells the angel controlling the video.

The video is again rewound and the small group are back inside the church, in their circle, with heads bowed. Annie forces herself not to smile as the people rush back along the pavement in reverse. *It's all so bizarre. To think that every detail of every person's life was being recorded.*

"Lord, I pray that souls might be saved through our outreach today. I pray that each leaflet will reach the right person and that You will prepare their hearts before-hand to receive the Message. Amen." A lady with a light green coat and dark hair.

"I pray that none of these leaflets would be wasted. That even if a person should discard one, it might be found and read by someone else…..."

Annie gasps as the video is paused again. "That's exactly what happened. That man threw the leaflet in the hedgerow and then the wind blew it to me and I read it!"

"Who do you think controls the wind, Annie?" Jesus asks.

"So that was really You bringing the leaflet to my attention?" Annie still can't believe it.

"It was in answer to the prayers of Jessica, Helen and all the other people who were praying for you." Jesus wants her to see how things really are.

"I didn't know how important it was though. If I'd known….how can You expect me to pay attention to one small piece of paper? That's not really fair." Annie is full of regrets but what she is saying seems reasonable, in her mind anyway.

"I'm afraid, Annie, that this is just one of fifteen Christian leaflets that you were offered in the street over the years. You took just five of them and, of these, four ended up in the nearest bin." An angel with a large book reads documented statistics.

Annie knows she is grasping at straws as she asks, "What happened to the fifth one?"

"You put it in your pocket and took it home," the angel says.

"And what happened to it?"Annie can't remember there ever being any Christian stuff in her house.

"Should we show her?" The angel looks at Jesus.

Jesus nods.

This time the scene is a living room in somebody's house.

"That's my house!" Annie exclaims. The familiarity is strangely comforting for a few seconds. "I thought you were going to show me what happened to the leaflet, though?"

"That's right," an angel confirms.

"But, this isn't the house I was living in when I was young. It's my house now...I mean....before I..." Annie can't bring herself to actually say the D word.

"Yes, Annie. The last leaflet you were offered was the one you took home," Jesus confirms.

Annie trembles, "How long ago was this?"

"I'm sorry Annie, it was just three months ago," Jesus says soberly.

Annie falls silent as she absorbs the shocking news. She had been given one last chance as recently as three months ago. "I did take the leaflet home, though. That's what you said, right?"

"Yes, that's right," Jesus answers. "Don't you remember this, Annie?"

Annie pales as she starts thinking about it. "Actually, I remember being given a leaflet. Yes, it was whilst I was wandering around in town. I was very upset about something. A young boy, only about fifteen, or sixteen, offered me the leaflet. When I refused it, he followed me along the street trying to give it to me. In the end, I decided it was easier just to take it to get rid of him."

"That's the one. That boy's name is Peter. He grew up in a care home, his parents both died in a car accident when he was only seven. Some Christians adopted him, when he was eleven, and taught him about Me," Jesus explains.

"So, if the leaflet ended up actually *in* my house, as You said, what happened to it?" Annie keeps coming back to this as she feels it must be significant somehow.

"You know this is important, don't you Annie?" Jesus asks.

"I think so, I don't really know why, I just sense that there's something special about that leaflet," Annie replies.

"You're right about that," an angel agrees.

The movie returns to the living room in Annie's family home. Annie's estranged husband Dean is sitting watching TV.

Annie flinches on seeing him, "Oh, so it's before the split. This could be awkward."

"We're looking for that leaflet remember Annie," Jesus reminds her.

A teenage girl comes racing down the stairs and into the living room. "Bye, Dad, I'm going out, okay?"

"Make sure you're back before ten, love." Dean pauses and looks at his daughter before fixing his gaze back on the TV.

Annie sees herself walk into the room. She sits down on a chair at a distance from her husband and picks up the remote. "Let's watch something else," she says as she flips the channel.

Dean's face tenses. He gets up and leaves the room.

"This was the difficult patch." Annie has no desire to rehash the bad memories but she doesn't seem to have a choice. "I thought this was about the leaflet?"

"Watch and see," an angel says.

The camera moves upstairs. A teenage boy is lounging on his bed. He's reading a book and listening to loud music at the same time.

"Grant, always listening to music. Could never get those headphones off him," Annie speaks wistfully as she thinks of her children. "I don't think I've ever seen him pick up a book, though. What is that?"

The camera zooms in and, as it pans around, the book cover is in focus. The title of the book is *Ultimate Questions*.

Is that a religious book? Where did he get it from and why would he read it? Grant was never interested in anything like that....

As they continue to watch Grant, he becomes sleepy and eventually, the small book falls on the floor as he leans back against the pillows and dozes off. A piece of paper also flutters to the floor and lands near the book.

That's more like Grant. The religious stuff obviously put him to sleep. Annie isn't surprised.

The camera zooms in again and the lens focuses on the floor. Firstly, it hovers over the book and then moves to the paper lying nearby.

"The leaflet?" Annie whispers. She is stunned. *Grant had it?*

A short clip appears on the screen at this point and shows Grant apparently creeping around the house at night. He goes downstairs and into a walk-in cupboard where the family hang their coats.

Annie again gasps as her son finds her black handbag, opens it and starts rummaging around. He pulls out her purse and takes several five-pound notes.

"He was stealing from me?" Annie asks.

"Afraid so, Annie. A lot of children steal from their parents these days. They seem to think it's their right to do so," an angel shakes his head sadly.

"Why are you showing me this, though?" Annie asks.

Grant puts the bag back on the hook but then hesitates. He gets the bag again and slides his hand into the large black pocket at the side of the bag.

"Crafty little…..that's where I kept loose change," Annie comments as if the angels need an explanation.

Grant pulls out a piece of paper and some coins. He glances at the paper then folds the coins inside it. He sneaks back upstairs to his room. He walks across to a small desk, switches on the light and tips the coins onto the table. He adds the five-pound notes and starts counting the money. The light shines on the slightly screwed up piece of paper and Annie reads the words, 'Where will you spend eternity?'

So, that's how the leaflet got there! I remember it now. I don't think I ever actually read it though, Annie tries to think back. *How did that lead to Grant reading religious books, though?*

As if she has again spoken out loud, the movie shows Grant at his desk writing something. Annie wants to see what it is, but it is obscured by his head and shoulders. He finishes writing and seals an envelope.

A few days later, a small parcel, addressed to Grant, arrives in the post.

Oh, did he write to someone to send it to him? Annie can't believe her son would have done this. He was only ever interested in music and football.

"Perhaps, you didn't know him as well as you thought, Annie?" an angel says.

Annie again thinks back, she remembers Grant disappearing on Sundays for the few weeks before her operation. She also recalls an odd conversation with him:

"Where are you going? It's pretty early for you to be up at the weekend, isn't it?" Annie had asked him.

"Just to see a few friends. No big deal Mum," Grant had answered.

Annie had been suspicious. It wasn't like Grant to get up early for anything or to be vague about where he was going. He tended to be honest about what he was up to even if his parents didn't like it.

She persisted, "Football friends?"

"Well, um, some of them play football, so yes, I guess so."

"Okay, well, remember that your father wanted to take you out this afternoon. You'd better be back in time as I really don't want any problems."

Annie winces as she realises how she had drawn her son into her marital struggles.

"Where did he go?" Annie snaps out of her daze and addresses the angels.

"Where do you think, Annie? You've seen that he was reading Christian books. Where do Christians go on Sundays?" The explanation is given in a patient tone.

"But, surely, Grant didn't seriously buy into all that, did he? Just from reading a piece of paper with a few words on it...." Annie is finding the whole thing hard to comprehend.

"It wasn't just a piece of paper Annie, it contained words from the Bible, words that God Himself wrote using human authors. When people read the Bible, God works in their hearts to convince them of its truth and importance," Jesus tells her.

"But, I've read bits of the Bible at school and in Sunday school. How come that didn't happen to me?" Annie is starting to move past the initial shock and now she wants explanations.

"Were you ever really paying attention, Annie? Did you ever read it in a sincere search for the truth?" Jesus prompts her.

"I guess not, but if the Bible is so powerful, then surely it would have got my attention anyway...."

Annie trails off as she realises that her argument is weak.

"There were times when you thought about what you were reading more seriously, and We began to show you truths, but as soon as you realised what was happening, you resisted and hardened your heart," Jesus reminds her.

Annie looks miserable. "Wait, so Grant actually became a Christian?"

"Let's see what happens," Jesus directs the angel towards the video controls once again.

The movie resumes. Grant is walking along a corridor with another boy who is carrying a football. They are laughing and joking. The other boy suddenly slaps Grant on the back in a friendly way and says, "You know what bro, you should come to the youth meeting on Friday."

Grant hesitates and flushes slightly red, "Is that a church thing? You know I'm not really into all that."

"It is at my church, yes, but the other kids are just like us. We'll probably just play football and then listen to a short talk."

"How long is the talk?" Grant looks suspiciously at his friend.

"Maybe five or ten minutes. You might learn something. What are you afraid of anyway? If you don't like it, then don't listen. At least you'll get to play football and the other kids are cool."

"Well, I guess it might be okay and if I don't like it I don't have to go again." Grant still sounds unsure.

"Great, I'll call round at your house on Friday and we can walk."

"Wait, what should I wear?" Grant suddenly asks.

"Doh, your kit, obviously."

"Oh, I thought it might be a suit and tie job." Grant feels a bit stupid but he really doesn't know what to expect.

The friend looks amused and a bubble appears above his head. *People's expectations of church are really strange…playing football in a suit and tie?!*

"See you Friday."

They part company.

"So, it wasn't just the leaflet," Annie says.

"Well, the leaflet got Grant's attention. Notice, though, that he didn't say anything to his friend about it," the angel observes.

"Why didn't he?" Annie is curious.

"Did you feel comfortable talking about religion with your friends?" Jesus asks. "It's one of the ways Satan keeps people away from the truth."

"What do you mean?" Annie is confused.

"He creates an environment where talking about religion is culturally inappropriate," Jesus explains.

"and death," an angel mutters.

"Yes, actually, that's true. People don't talk about these things anymore. It's incredible really when they are so important and so much is at stake. Wait, though, who is Satan?"

"It's one of the names for the devil," Jesus tells her.

"You mean the red creature with horns and a pitch fork? You

can't expect me to believe that he's real." Annie stares, incredulous.

"It's one of his best tricks. To make people think of him as a fictional creature akin to a fairy or goblin. Then he can do his best, or worst, work undetected. Believe me, he definitely exists and he is responsible for a lot of the destruction and pain in the world."

"But, why don't you stop him then?" Annie asks an obvious question.

"He will be stopped, but not until the end," Jesus answers.

Chapter 2

Annie jumps as a loud sound startles her. She turns towards the sound and sees some more angels emerging from a small door. They are busily arranging another screen that has dropped down from the ceiling. That must have caused the loud noise. Annie looks questioningly towards those she had been speaking to.

"You asked whether Grant became a Christian. I thought it might be helpful for you to see what is happening on Earth now. There is no time here, so we can see what is happening at any point in the present or the future, but your eyes will be restricted to the present, Annie," Jesus informs her.

A picture appears on the screen. A church full of people wearing black, many are crying and a coffin is making its way down the centre aisle.

Annie gasps, "Grant died?! But he was even younger than me."

"No, Annie," an angel assures her. "Look, there's Grant."

Annie sees Grant and Sophie, her two children, and sighs with relief. Then she sees her estranged husband Dean. The three of them are sitting together at the front of the church. All are sobbing.

"Whose funeral is it then? It must be someone that was close to us as a family." Annie can't figure it out. The family tended to keep themselves to themselves as far as possible. "Oh, it must be one of Dean's parents, but then, why would Grant be crying, he never got on well with them. One of my parents, then? But, Dean couldn't stand them, especially since the separation, and he's crying too." Annie looks blankly at the angels.

"Come on, Annie. Remember there's no time here. Whose death would impact your family in this way?" Jesus prompts.

"Oh….," Annie says softly as the truth hits her. "It's my funeral. I'm not sure I want to watch this. It could be very weird."

"It's important for you to see the legacy you left," Jesus tells her.

Annie senses that it isn't optional, and she is happy to delay the inevitable end of this examination of her life.

"Look, Annie, do you see who else is there," an angel asks. He pauses the video and points to several figures towards the back of the church.

Annie doesn't recognise the two ladies but one of them looks vaguely familiar. "Who are they?" she eventually asks after staring and racking her brain, for a short time.

"You've already seen them today, on the other video, Annie," the angel prompts. "But they were a little younger then."

"Wait, oh, I guess it must be Helen and, um, is it Jessica?" Annie asks, she still isn't sure.

"Yes, that's right."

"I lost touch with them years ago, why would they even bother coming to my funeral?" Annie is surprised, she knows that she wouldn't have shown such concern for her former friends had things been the other way around.

"Grant found some details in an old diary of yours and decided they might want to come," Jesus tells her. "Right, let's watch this part."

Silence reigns and every eye is fixed on the screen as a man in black robes and a clerical collar moves to the front of the church and stands behind the lectern which holds a large black Bible. He begins to pray in a loud voice and everyone in the church bows their heads. Most close their eyes, apart from a few wide-eyed children who glance around. The prayer is long and full of words that Annie doesn't understand.

"Bless our sister Annabelle Yale and receive her soul into Thy heavenly dwelling places. Remove the curse of Satan and purge her of all uncleanness. Bring comfort to her remaining family and surround them with love, peace and unity in the Spirit......" The minister drones on and heads start to nod around the church.

"No wonder I didn't get on with this religious stuff, it doesn't make any sense to me, even now," Annie whispers.

Jesus nods. He looks disappointed.

The minister finishes his lengthy prayer with an 'amen' which is dutifully repeated by most people in the congregation.

"Now, we are going to sing a special request from some members of Annabelle's family. Please turn to page four in your service sheet."

I wonder which song they chose. Annie feels an inexplicable dread as the camera zooms in on one of the service sheets and she reads the words:

"For what is a man, what has
he got
If not himself, then he has naught
To say the things he truly feels
And not the words of one who kneels
The record shows I took the blows
And did it my way.

Yes, it was my way."

She immediately recognises the final lyrics of her favourite song, *My Way* by Frank Sinatra, and the irony isn't lost on her.

"Are they really going to sing this in a church?" Annie is ashamed and embarrassed, despite having nothing to do with the decision. She hangs her head as the congregation sing the favourite song with gusto, seemingly oblivious to the atheistic lyrics. Annie raises her head slightly as the song draws to a close, she looks at the body of people. She notices that a few aren't singing. These people, although few in number, are significant to Annie as they include Grant, Jessica and Helen. Their heads are bowed as if in silent prayer, and the expressions on their faces are sombre.

At the end of the song, the minister, who had been singing along cheerfully, announces that a few people will be saying some words before the sermon. He promises to keep his message brief, as he knows people probably have other things planned for later in the day. On hearing these words, there is almost an audible sigh of relief from the large body of people.

Dean walks to the front of the church and reads a loving tribute to his "fun-loving, hard-working, wife, who died far too young."

Annie snorts as she hears his words. "Who does he think he's fooling, we'd been separated for two months already and he'd already served the papers." Annie feels a strong desire to justify herself as if this will somehow make a difference to her predicament. She realises, at the same time, that a lot of the people in attendance probably didn't yet know about their marriage struggles. Dean's behaviour still seems fake and insincere. However, Annie knows deep down that she would most likely have done the same thing had circumstances been reversed. *I mean, who wants personal struggles to be dredged up when someone has already died. Don't speak ill of the dead...or something like that.*

Dean concludes with the words, "May my dear wife, Annie, be carried away with the angels to heaven and rest in peace."

Annie blinks, *If only they knew.*

"Isn't anyone going to say something religious? After all, they are in church!" she asks a little desperately.

Jesus and the angels remain silent.

The minister resumes his position behind the lectern. The Bible remains closed. He begins speaking, "We are gathered here today to remember the life of Annabelle Yale who was suddenly taken from us last week. We know that she lived a good, moral life and was married to Dean until the day of her death. She blessed many of those around her and was involved in charity work. She followed the example of Jesus who took pity on the poor and destitute."

"Wait, when did I do charity work?" Annie is astonished. She can't recall any such thing. In fact, she had always thought that voluntary work was a waste of time and that people only did it because they couldn't get proper jobs.

"Dean told him about the time you worked in Oxfam," an angel says after examining a large scroll.

"That was paid, I managed the shop and it was only for a few weeks!!" Annie is horrified by the misrepresentation. "And, I left because the money wasn't good enough," her voice has become a whisper.

Annie listens as her list of positive attributes continues to be embellished by the minister who is doing his best to make people remember Annie fondly.

She feels sick to her stomach. The façade is truly appalling and she wants it to stop. She spins away from the screen, falls to her knees and tries to hide her face.

"We know that God accepts those who are sincere and try to live a good life. Annie did this and we can be sure she will be celebrating in heaven with Jesus at this moment." The minister speaks boldly and seems to be full of confidence.

Annie crawls away from the screen sobbing.

There is a murmur in the congregation as Grant stands up. He moves towards the minister, who has just finished speaking and appears about to announce another song. There is tension and determination on Grant's face. His fists are clenched by his side. He whispers a few words to the minister who nods and quickly steps aside. He pales slightly.

Grant steps in front of the lectum and opens the large black Bible.

"Annie, I think you should watch this," Jesus tells her.

Annie is strangely compelled to crawl back to the screen.

Grant begins reading, his voice is shaky but the words are clear, "Jesus said, 'I am the way, the truth and the life, no one comes to the Father except through Me.' These are the words of Jesus, from the Bible, and they apply to each one of us. None of us can approach God in our current state because He is perfectly holy and we are full of sin. Thankfully, God had a rescue plan. He sent Jesus, His Son, to live a perfect life and to die in our place and for our sin. Believing this is the only way to get to heaven. Living a good life and being sincere won't cut it because none of us could do enough good things or be sincere enough. We aren't perfect. Without Jesus, we will be punished for our sin when we die in a place called hell, forever."

There is complete silence as people hang on every word from the son of the lady lying in the coffin at the front of the church.

A chair loudly scrapes as Dean stands then storms down the aisle and out of the church. He casts a disgusted glance at his son as he makes his dramatic exit.

Grant hesitates, just for a second, before continuing his speech. "Perhaps, some of you are thinking this is completely inappropriate. To bring religion into the mix at a time when people are grieving. Let me ask you, though. What is more loving, for me to warn you before it's too late for you as well, or to hold off for fear of being culturally inappropriate? I'm convinced that my mum would want me to do this. I only wish I had warned her and I will have to live with that guilt for the rest of my life." Tears stream down Grant's face as he retakes his seat. Sophie sits rigidly beside him, a mixture of fear and shock frozen on her face.

Annie wants to reach out to her son and wipe the tears away, but she knows it's too late. She feels pain, and regret, at what might have been.

The minister, who had taken a seat after Grant's interruption, suddenly realises that he is expected to continue the service. He is now a whiter shade of pale as he moves awkwardly towards the platform. Should he acknowledge the complete contradiction of all he had said, or just breeze past it and carry on? He decides on the latter, anything for an easy life.

"Well, that was quite a speech. Thankyou for your honesty, young man. I'm sure you are hurting and grieving the loss of your mother, as are many others here. Right, let's sing our final song, number one on your sheet, *Amazing Grace.*"

The familiar music begins, but the congregation are subdued as they sing. Gone is the joyful enthusiasm that had been evident for Sinatra's most famous song. They are now collectively forced to think about their own eternal destiny in the words of John Newton:

> *"Amazing grace! How sweet the sound*
> *That saved a wretch like me.*

I once was lost, but now am found,
Was blind, but now I see.

'Twas grace that taught my
heart to fear,
And grace my fears relieved.
How precious did that grace appear
The hour I first believed.

Through many dangers, toils
and snares
I have already come;
'Tis grace hath brought me safe thus
far
And grace will lead me home.

The Lord has promised good to
me
His word my hope secures;
He will my shield and portion be,
As long as life endures.

Yea, when this flesh and heart
shall fail,
and mortal life shall cease,
I shall possess within the veil
A life of joy and peace.

When we've been there ten
thousand years
Bright shining as the sun,
We've no less days to sing God's

praise
Than when we've first begun."

Grant's sobering message has brought sudden clarity to these lyrics for many in the congregation for the first time. They find they are unable to sing as the words don't apply to them. They stutter and stumble and feel utterly miserable, desperate for any type of distraction...and for the service to end. Even for those who happily go along to carol services at Christmas, and sing lustily at Easter, it now feels hypocritical to utter such significant things without the sincerity to back it up.

Heads go down as the minister prays the final prayer, then most people jump up and quickly head for the exit. A few remain seated as if held by glue. They look stunned.

Grant looks around, having composed himself and wishes he had ensured a Christian minister would be taking the service and not just someone paid to do a job. He feels inadequate to deal with the few remaining people who are most likely in need of some advice, and help, relating to what they've heard. Gratefully, he watches Helen and Jessica and a few others as they approach them.

There is an older man still sitting alone at the back of the church. Grant braces himself as he begins the long walk down the aisle. It is only when he is beyond the point of being able to turn back that he realises it's his paternal grandfather. *Oh no, they never really liked me and now I've probably seriously offended them. Perhaps, I shouldn't talk to him.* Grant pauses as his grandfather looks up and, as if seeing him for the first time, beckons for him to approach.

Grant prepares for a serious telling off, or disinheritance, or any other likely scenario, but his feet propel him forward. He slides into the pew next to his grandfather and notices the tear tracks on his weary face. They sit in silence for a minute.

Annie is now watching the film earnestly. She has no idea how Dean's father will respond to Grant. Their relationship had always been difficult, but strange things have already happened and anything is possible.

"I just want to know one thing," the older man finally speaks.

"What is it, Granddad?" Grant asks with trepidation.

"Why?"

"I felt I had to do it," Grant answers as best he can.

"I don't understand. There's nothing in it for you. You risked losing your family and friends to comment on the life of someone who's already died. Why would you do that?" He seems genuinely perplexed.

"It wasn't for my mum, it's too late for her. It's because I really believe it's true and that all people will one day stand before God and will have to give an account of their life. Then they will be sent to heaven or hell, forever, depending on whether or not their sin has been dealt with," Grant finishes and holds his breath, waiting for the rebuke that he knows must be coming. His grandfather is of a generation where it is considered disrespectful to talk down to elders.

"Hmm, so what you're saying is that you're willing to sacrifice your own reputation and relationships for the sake of your beliefs because you care more for these people than you do about yourself."

Grant can see the wheels turning in his grandfather's head. A Bible verse suddenly pops into his mind, "The Bible puts it like this, *'For what shall it profit a man if he gains the whole world yet loses his own soul,'* Most people think in terms of giving up money or things, but it can apply to anything we have on Earth, including our reputations and relationships."

"I remembered some of the things you said in your speech today from when I was a child. It struck an odd nerve in me. Could it be true?"

"Darling, are you coming, we're going to be late…." the shrill sound of Grant's grandmother cuts through the reverie.

Grant remains silent as his grandfather jumps in response to his wife's call, then stands, and, shaking his head in bewilderment, makes his way out of the church. Grant bows his head in prayer.

Annie watches the scene in amazement. She feels a mixture of pride on witnessing the behaviour of her son, and sorrow at her own impending doom. "At least some good came out of my death," she comments.

"There are numerous funerals every day without a mention of God, and plenty of others where He is central in name only. That would have been the case at your funeral as well if it weren't for Grant. It's another trick of the devil, convincing people they can pay lip service to God, or just acknowledge Him at weddings and funerals, or Christmas and Easter, then forget about Him for the rest of the year. What kind of Deity accepts that kind of haphazard and insincere worship, though?" Jesus' words force Annie to think.

"A pathetic, powerless one, desperate for attention," Annie mumbles.

"Right, and you've touched on another of the enemy's tactics; he presents God as a weakling more in need of people than they are of Him. He convinces them that they can behave how they like and do whatever they want because God's love will over-ride their every failure without the need for repentance on their part."

"Yes, I can see that now. I guess that's why I sat on the fence for so long. I had no real understanding, or fear, of God, and Who He truly is," Annie speaks wistfully. "Wait, though, you said that hearing the truth doesn't guarantee a positive response from people. What happened to Dean's father after he left the church?"

"What do you mean, what happened?" Jesus asks her.

"Well, he heard the Message and it touched his heart, he even asked whether it could be true." Annie increasingly senses the urgency of the task on Earth despite being unable to rescue herself.

"Rewind the film slightly," Jesus instructs.

The film is rewound. It shows the old man standing up, about to leave.

"Just pause it there," Jesus says.

"Did you see that Annie?"

"What, you mean, when he shook his head?" Annie asks puzzled.

"That was his dismissal of everything he had just heard and seen. He basically thought about it whilst he was sitting there, but then pushed it out of his mind and heart, once and for all, with that shake of his head. Then he walked away from the light, which was attempting to bring the Truth home to him, by walking away from Grant, and out of the church. Notice that he doesn't even look back. He won't think about that service or anything that happened that day, again," Jesus solemnly tells her.

"How can a person do that, though?" Annie asks.

"Years of deliberately hardening his heart to the Truth. It would truly take a miracle to break through all those layers and sadly he doesn't want to hear it. He will make sure now that he doesn't put himself in a position again where he hears about Me," Jesus says.

"There's more, Annie. Every time the Word of God is clearly

preached, there will be responses, some positive and some negative. Grant had the courage to present the whole Message, we are watching the responses. Look...."

Annie looks again at the big screen as the images move forward. Dean's grandfather walks out of the church and they again watch Grant bow his head in prayer. As he lifts his head a few minutes later, there is a soft whimper coming from nearer the front of the church. Grant looks perplexed as he stands and hurries back to his former seat. Sophie is leaning forward and has her head in her hands. She is crying softly.

"Oh, I thought you'd left already..." Grant looks slightly awkward as he hovers over his younger sister.

Her head snaps up as she hears his voice, "I didn't know you were still here," Sophie says.

"I was talking to grand-dad at the back of the church, but he's gone now," Grant explains. "Are you okay? Just sad about Mum?"

"I am sad about Mum, but what you said and did shocked me," Sophie cries.

"Why? You've heard the things I said before," Grant replies.

"I know, I just didn't realise how serious you were about it all or that it might actually be true. It made me think about my own life and whether I could be in danger. What made you start to take it all so seriously?"

"It's a long story, but basically, I read a leaflet that made me think, then a friend at school invited me to a youth group. I kept hearing the same things about Jesus and in time I realised it must be true. Then, I knew that I needed God to forgive the things I'd done wrong that had been troubling me for a long time. I asked God to forgive me for those things and trusted that He would because Jesus was punished for them on the cross. Then, I started to live a new life following Jesus."

"What, just like that?" Sophie sounds amazed. "It can't be that simple, can it?"

"Well, yes, it's simple in one way, but life as a Christian is difficult because you'll always be going in the opposite direction to everyone else. You have to really believe in your heart that it's true, that Jesus died on the cross to pay the price for your sin. Otherwise, when things get difficult, you'll just give up." Grant sits down next to his sister.

"So, if I tell God I'm sorry for my sin and follow Jesus, I'll go to heaven one day? That's what you said, right?" Sophie asks somewhat shyly.

"Yes, that's what the Bible teaches," Grant is surprised by his sister's sudden interest in Christianity.

"Seems like there's nothing to lose." Sophie wipes away her tears and starts to smile. "What do I need to do?"

"Take some time to pray to God, ask forgiveness for the things you've done wrong, then resolve to try not to do those things again, then live a new life following Jesus," Grant says carefully.

A bubble appears above his head, *It's great that she's showing so much interest, but I wonder how sincere she is and whether it's just surface level due to her emotional state right now.*

Annie watches the scene curiously. "Sophie too? Wow, that's great!"

"I'm sorry, Annie. Not all those who seem to profess faith actually follow it through," an angel explains.

The video skips forward and another scene appears. There are three girls walking together along a school corridor. Sophie is heading towards them from the other direction. As she walks past the girls one of them sticks out a foot and she trips over. Her books fall to the floor.

"Bible-basher," one of the three girls sneers at her.

"Think you're better than us, Little Miss Holy," another of the girls stands over her as she collects her books.

A bubble appears above Sophie's head, *I wish I could just fit in, it's too hard all this Christian stuff. I'd rather be popular with lots of friends. Perhaps, it's not too late as I've only just started this school and not many of them know I've been going to church.*

The scene ends and the monitor powers down.

"What? That's it?" Annie exclaims. "Surely, it took more than that for my daughter to abandon something she seemed so sure about only a few weeks before."

"I'm afraid Sophie wasn't prepared for the trouble that comes to people who believe in Me," Jesus says. "When she first heard that her sin could be forgiven and she could have a new start, she was excited and happy to go along with what Grant said. However, she didn't really count the cost of following Me. In the end, she chose the easier path preferring to blend in with her friends. She is still young, though, and there may be other opportunities for her.

"Can I see what happens to her?" Annie asks almost desperately.

"No, Annie. I said that your view will be limited to the present. This exercise is not to satisfy your curiosity, but to help you to see that your punishment is just and fair. In relation to Sophie, you were responsible for teaching her the right path in life, but sadly you failed. You didn't teach her about Me or the Bible and God wasn't even mentioned in your house until Grant started his investigation."

Annie knows that this failure will be added to her growing list. How she wishes she had looked at life differently and paid attention to those who were trying to tell her how things really were. Instead, she had sneered at, and shunned, everyone who had tried to help her.

"Okay, Annie, there was another person impacted by your funeral. Shall we look at what happened there?" an angel asks.

Annie likes the idea of a subject change and knows the angel is referring to Dean, "I guess so, Dean looked pretty furious when he left the church."

Images again appear on the screen. Dean is storming out of the church and heading for his car in the car park outside. His face is red and his fists clenched by his side. He gets in the driver's seat and puts his foot down. A bubble appears above the vehicle as he speeds along. *How dare he? Who does he think he is to judge us? I can't believe Grant is my son. Well, not anymore. That's the last time I speak to him.* He continues along the road and just manages to stop for a red light. *I'd better calm down a little, if I want to get home in one piece.* He waits at the light. *What if Grant was right?, I've heard those things about Jesus before, a long time ago. Wait, where did that thought come from?*

Dean accelerates and immediately spots an Off Licence. *I need a drink.* He pulls the car over, heads inside and grabs a case of beer. The thought of a few drinks cheers him up as he continues his journey.

He arrives home and adds the lager to the fridge which is already full of alcohol. He pops open a drink and takes a big swig feeling slightly better straight away. *I'll show them, I won't turn up for the burial, then they'll wonder where I am and he'll be sorry. I did my best not to embarrass the family or air our dirty laundry in public but I shouldn't have bothered. Grant ruined everything anyway.* ***HOW DARE HE!***

Dean finishes his first beer and grabs another one from the fridge. He lies down on the sofa and flicks on the TV. He can't focus, though, as thoughts continue running through his head. *How did Grant get so involved in all of this stuff anyway? It seemed like he was really serious about it....what if it is true?*

The film abruptly ends.

"Wait, I want to see what happens next," Annie exclaims.

Jesus looks at the angel holding the remote and nods. The film starts up again.

Dean glances down at a pile of paperwork on the coffee table in front of him. He picks it up and starts sorting through it absent-mindedly. He casts his eyes over the divorce papers and Annie's will. *Well, at least now I'll own the whole house and both cars. It was definitely a good idea to take out that life insurance policy last year. I need to check how much it was for. Might be enough to have a few extra holidays this year and to build an extension. I could even go on that cruise I've been wanting to do for years. If I did it with a singles group, I might even meet someone. Perhaps, it's not so bad after all. In fact, it might be the easiest way out of this whole situation as people won't even need to know our marriage was in trouble. I can walk away and start again with more money and a lot more freedom, no more nagging and complaining.....*

The film freezes with the thought bubble over Dean's head.

"What? So, he didn't do anything about what he heard at the funeral. Surely he would have wanted to look into it to see whether or not it was true?!" Annie can't believe it.

"He considered it, but the desire for money and other material things distracted him and then became his immediate focus….." Jesus says.

"Did he ever become a Christian?" Annie isn't sure why she is asking the question about her estranged husband, or why she even cares, but she is becoming increasingly aware that the only thing that really matters about a person's time on Earth is whether or not they trusted Jesus by the time of their death.

"That's not for you to know Annie," Jesus reminds her. "We are reviewing your life, not the life of others. Only I know the future."

Chapter 3

We're going to continue looking at your life now," Jesus announces.

Annie falls silent. She doesn't want to watch any more humiliating experiences on the big screen. She has long since realised that any good that she thought she had done was minute, and mostly selfishly motivated.

"I want to address some of the things you've said so far, Annie," Jesus says. "We've already looked at the opportunities you had to learn about Me through your childhood friends, and leaflets being given to you in the street. Actually, though, that's the tip of the iceberg. Don't you remember the period you went to church for a while?" Jesus already knows the answer, of course, but wants Annie to remember.

"Not really, why would I have done that?" Annie asks. "Oh, do you mean at Christmas and Easter? Of course, I went then, with everyone else."

"I know you went then, but there was also a time where you went every week for a while. It was when you were at university," Jesus gives her a few more details.

"Oh yeah, now I remember, I somehow got involved in the Christian Union and went to church as I thought it might look good on my CV," Annie admits

"That was one of the reasons, but do you remember the real reason you went along?" Jesus replies.

"Not really," Annie knows it can't be good as the angels start shifting uncomfortably as if preparing for something terrible that's about to be exposed. "Hold on, though, I thought from all that's been said so far that church attendance isn't enough." The thought suddenly occurs to Annie and she blurts it out hoping for a subject change.

"You're right, Annie. Being a Christian isn't about church attendance, but we are looking at the opportunities you had to hear and respond to Me," Jesus says.

"If the main message is the same thing Grant said at my funeral,

I don't remember hearing that before," Annie comments.

"You have heard the Truth many times, Annie," Jesus tells her. "Let's watch."

The original screen comes to life again. Annie is now in her early twenties and is sitting on a sofa in a house. She is earnestly talking to a man.

"That's Daniel. What's he got to do with this?" Annie asks.

"Oh good, you remember him. Unfortunately, he wasn't a good influence on you," Jesus says. "The devil used him to manipulate you."

Daniel says to Annie, "If you really like him, you'll have to convince him you're into in all that religious stuff. That's the only way. It's all he's interested in these days."

"But, I'm really not interested in religion, isn't that wrong?" Annie asks.

"Depends how much you want to be with him, I'm telling you, Annie, he won't date a non-believer."

"I don't think I can fake it, though," Annie protests.

"Of course you can, we're all wearing masks. You can be whoever you want to be. Just do some research and learn enough to convince him. Then go to church for a while and throw a few Bible verses in. He'll be smitten," Daniel grins.

"What happens when he finds out?" Annie asks.

"By then, he'll be in love and he won't care," Daniel says cruelly. "Besides you'll be doing him, and me, a favour, as all that religion stuff is nonsense anyway and it's taken over his life. He's such a bore now."

The angels shake their heads, "It catches so many people out," one of them says.

"You're right, I'll do it. I do really like him," Annie says as she gives in.

I can't believe I agreed to do that. To try and derail someone's sincere beliefs for my own selfish gain. What's wrong with me?

"I guess it didn't work?" she asks Jesus, almost pleadingly.

"Watch and see," Jesus says. "You're right, that this is not your finest hour, Annie, by anyone's standards."

The movie flashes through clips of Annie attending church and CU meetings, making a big show of being involved in Christian charity work, and publicly giving money. Annie is totally humiliated as she knows the motivations of her heart are on display for all to see. The video also catches the sideways glances at Jason, the object of her affection, to see if he is watching her religious sincerity and good deeds.

Once again, Annie feels ill.

"I think we've seen enough of that," Jesus instructs.

The movie jumps forward a few months. Jason is walking towards Annie with an odd expression on his face. She waits expectantly.

"Annie, I've been praying about this for a while now and have spoken to our pastor about it. I wondered if you wanted to go out to dinner with me later this week?"

Annie's face flushes and a bright smile lights up her face, "I've been praying too and I think this is exactly what God wants. Yes, I'd love to go."

Jason smiles back, "Great, how about Friday? I can pick you up?"

"Yes, sounds good," Annie replies.

Watching her younger self, Annie remembers the twinge of guilt she felt at that very moment, how she suppressed it and convinced herself it would be worth it in the end. She remembers rushing off shopping to make sure she had a new outfit for the date with Jason. She remembers buying the most revealing clothes that she could get away with as a 'Christian'. Clothes that would really show off her body and make Jason like her even more. Her friends encouraged her as they tried clothes on together and laughed at the thought of poor Jason having taken on more than he could handle. Looking back, it all seems so wrong. Annie can't quite remember what happened on the actual date, though.

The video shows Annie, on the eve of their date, opening the front door in response to the bell. Jason is standing there with a bunch of flowers and a big smile. He looks her up and down briefly, then averts his eyes as his smile falters and he hides behind the flowers.

"These are for you," he mumbles, thrusting them towards her and stepping backwards. "You should grab a coat, it's cold outside."

"It's not too cold, besides, I want to show off my new dress," Annie answers. She wants Jason to know that she's made a special effort for him.

Jason doesn't look at her as they head out of the door and Annie notices that he is keeping his distance. She feels a little uncomfortable but shakes it off as first date nerves.

"I thought we'd go somewhere relaxed and informal. I hope that's okay?" Jason says this in a way that makes it clear he's already decided.

"As long as I'm not going to stand out like a sore thumb in these clothes," Annie comments.

Jason bites his lip and says nothing.

Annie notices that Jason is smartly dressed but looks similar to how he always looks at church.

They pause outside Nando's. Annie blinks. *Surely not?* She breathes a sigh of relief as Jason keeps driving, he's barely said a word to her.

"Right, here we are," he speaks brightly but his voice falters.

Annie looks up and sees the Nando's sign, closer now. Jason must've spun the car around and entered from the other side.

Jason jumps out and heads for the front door of the restaurant as Annie is forced to scramble to catch up with him.

What on earth is wrong?

Jason waits for Annie at the entrance and holds the door for her stiffly as if they are strangers. He has an odd expression plastered on his face, one that Annie doesn't recognise.

They find a table and order their food. Jason barely says a word and Annie grows increasingly uncomfortable….

"I think we've seen enough of this. Annie, do you remember the date now?" Jesus asks.

"Yes, it was terrible. I don't want to watch any more," Annie replies softly.

"We don't need to see any more of the actual date, but I think you need to know why Jason behaved like that," Jesus says.

The screen flickers. Jason is now huddled with two of his friends, Matt and Simon, in a booth, in a restaurant..

"I didn't know what to do, honestly. It was our first date, but when she showed up looking like that and refused to even wear a coat, it was like she was a different person. I realised straight away that it would never work between us if she thinks it's okay to go out dressed like that." Jason looks miserable as he explains to his friends what happened on his first date with Annie.

"Woah, man. That's a bit hasty. Couldn't you just tell her how it makes you feel?" Matt advises.

"I might have done, but I've got the horrible feeling that she did it on purpose knowing exactly how it would make me feel." Jason looks at his two friends. "In fact, I'm starting to wonder whether that was her goal all along."

"What do you mean?" Simon is confused.

"Well, she hasn't been in church long and she was very keen when I asked her out," Jason says. "What if she's been making a play for me the whole time...."

"Really, do you think she would go to that much trouble, for a date with you?" Matt looks doubtful.

"The devil works in subtle ways," Jason says in a subdued tone.

"Why don't you give her the benefit of the doubt?" Simon suggests.

"I just don't think I can trust her now. I think I'll see whether she sticks around at church even if I don't ask her out again," Jason says thoughtfully. *How could I have been so stupid?*

Annie watches the rest of the clip with her hands partially covering her face. *Oh no, I'm so embarrassed.*

"You stopped going to church and CU when you realised he wasn't interested," an angel tells her.

"I know, I remember it well now. I just thought Jason wasn't sure how to conduct himself on the date, or that he was nervous, or something," Annie still can't believe what she's just seen.

"I'm afraid it gets worse Annie. Jason had been honestly praying about you, as he said. You lied to him when you told him you had also been praying. We actually stepped in and prevented things going any further to protect Jason, and to put an end to your deception," Jesus gives her the final details.

"A willing tool in the enemy's hands," an angel sighs.

"So, I guess that was my last appearance in church?" Annie asks.

"Where did you get married, Annie?" Jesus reminds her.

"Oh, of course. I meant when I didn't *have* to be there," Annie flushes as she realises what she's just said.

"It's not an excuse, Annie, but sadly, most people think of church in the same way. Just somewhere to go for official occasions rather than a place to worship God," Jesus tells her.

"We did look at a humanist wedding, or just having the registry office ceremony, but it didn't seem like it would be a real wedding if it wasn't in a church," Annie reminisces.

"It probably would have been better if you hadn't got married in a church seeing as neither of you believed in God," an angel comments sternly. "Actually, it's not the building that matters but the fact that you made vows before a God you didn't believe in, and your service included Bible verses that you didn't believe were true. It was insincere from the outset."

"I didn't think about it like that," Annie says soberly.

"Why not? Would you think it was okay to sign a contract clearly stating principles you didn't agree with? Or make a vow that you knew you couldn't keep?" an angel asks her.

"But, we changed our vows to make them more relevant to us," Annie protests.

"Yes, you cut out the requirement for you to obey your husband, but do you remember what you vowed to do instead?"

"Um, I think I said I would love, honour and cherish," Annie guesses.

"Actually, you just said, love and cherish," an angel reads from a scroll.

Annie wonders how many scrolls there are if her every word has been recorded. Then she considers how many scrolls there must be if every word ever said by every person has been taken down for later scrutiny. It's a scary thought.

"That's right, now I remember," Annie agrees. *What's wrong with that? I just got rid of the sexist, dated language. Surely, they don't object to that.*

"Annie, what was the rest of the sentence?" the angel asks.

"I don't really remember, something about, 'til death do us

part?" Annie doesn't understand why this is so significant. She hadn't intended her marriage to break down and had been sincere when she made her vows....

"You actually said this;

I, Annie, take you, Dean, to be my husband, to have and to hold from this day forward, for better, for worse, for richer, for poorer, in sickness and in health, to love and to cherish, till death us do part, according to God's holy law, and this is my solemn vow,"

Jesus tells her.

"Yes, that sounds familiar. What's the problem, though? Is this about our separation? That wasn't our intention. We just had irreconcilable differences in the end," Annie says.

"Whilst it's sad that your marriage broke down, that's not the point that's being made here Annie. Look closely at your wedding vow," an angel points to the screen as the words appear in big letters.

The angel produces a long wooden stick and moves it along under the words as Annie reads aloud. When he gets to the last line, he pauses.

"Oh!" Annie exclaims. "I made the vow to do all these things according to God's holy law but I didn't even believe in God! My whole marriage was a sham…."

"Right, Annie. The Bible is routinely used as an instrument to ensure the appearance of truth as people swear on it in court rooms up and down the land, yet these same people abhor the content. Don't you see the hypocrisy and meaninglessness of all of these procedures?" Jesus asks her.

"I do, now. Why doesn't someone say something? Why don't they realise that it's all so wrong?" Annie's eyes have suddenly been opened to the lunacy on Earth; empty rituals in the name of a God that most either never believed in in the first place, have long since abandoned, or have given up as a fairy story.

"I hate hypocrisy, Annie; people that honour Me with their lips when their hearts are far from Me," Jesus says.

"Do you remember how you managed to secure your church wedding in the first place?" an angel asks.

Oh no, it can't get any worse, can it?

"Unfortunately, yes," an angel says.

"I remember going to a few services at the church before the wedding," Annie is vague again as it's all a bit of a blur.

"Yes, you did marriage classes and lied your way through the vicar's questions. You even became members of the church," an angel says.

"I hadn't realised there would be so many questions, or so much involved in getting married. I remember that I felt uncomfortable, but it felt like it was too late to back out and that we should just keep going and get through the procedure," Annie finishes lamely, "Oh, and I asked a few of my friends who said they had gone through the same thing, and that the church expected people to lie. They said it didn't matter as long as I was sincere in wanting to get married….." Annie trails off completely as she realises how utterly ridiculous her excuses now sound.

"Annie, this vicar, who is a real servant of Mine, a Christian, asked you whether you were sleeping together and various other relevant questions about your faith and intentions. You were actually living together, and you were several weeks pregnant when you started the classes, you had no intention of being involved in church beyond the wedding, and you had no faith to speak of. How can you possibly reconcile any of that with the answers you and Dean gave to the vicar? Would you have lied like that in any other area of your life?" Jesus asks and waits for an answer.

"It didn't feel like it was really lying, just that we had to do what was necessary so that we could get married. Every situation is different after all," Annie squirms in her chair.

"Do you think the vicar would have married you if he had known the reality?" Jesus asks her.

"I don't know," Annie says softly.

Jesus shakes his head. "Oh, Annie. I can see I'm going to have to make things crystal clear. Let me show you what happened after your wedding."

The screen flickers to life. They are watching the vicar alone in his office at the back of his church. He is praying. A book is open in front of him on the desk. The camera zooms in and Annie sees that it contains lists of names with dates and contact details. She sees her own name listed along with her former husband's. The page is headed 'weddings'. There is an empty column at the edge of the page and at the top of the column is written 'church attendance'. Annie watches as the vicar scans the list and shakes his head before closing his eyes once more, and resuming his solitary prayer.

"I don't get it, "Annie says.

"Annie, you and Dean became members of this vicar's church when he agreed to conduct your wedding. You signed a membership agreement stating that you would regularly attend services and take part in the life of the church. You even submitted a written testimony explaining how you became a Christian which reassured the vicar that you were genuine," an angel says.

"But, how did I know what to say?" Annie is increasingly horrified by the way she has duped this sincere old man.

"You copied a testimony off the internet and found one for Dean as well," Jesus says. "Again, I have to ask whether you would have done this in any other area of your life. Doesn't it seem wrong, Annie?"

"I don't remember this. I guess, though, that others did the same thing as the 'church attendance' box is empty all the way down the page," Annie hopes she can redeem herself slightly by blending in with the crowd.

"Do you think that those who commit fraud and are never caught by the police are any better than those who get caught and are punished?" Jesus asks her.

"Oh….." the point hits home.

"The old man must've realised that people would just say what he wanted to hear, though, surely," Annie grasps at a straw.

"There are a lot of vicars who just want to go through the motions, yes. However, this man sincerely wanted to do the right thing and only to marry those who were genuine Christians, and wanted to join his church. He was devastated to find a whole batch of people willing to lie and dupe him into conducting their ceremonies. In fact, he spent a long time wondering where he had gone wrong when the various couples didn't show up at his church. In the end, he withdrew completely and resigned from the ministry," an angel is reading again from a scroll.

"What happened to him in the end?" Annie asks dreading the answer.

"He became disillusioned for a while, and depressed, but after a few years, he picked himself back up and found a job in a shop. He started going to a different church and his relationship with Me was restored," Jesus tells her.

"I can't believe my actions could have such a big effect on someone," Annie is appalled by her behaviour and full of regret.

"As this man was a true believer, he wasn't ever in danger of falling away from Me completely, he just took a knock, but he's safe forever now," Jesus adds. "He died a few years after your wedding."

Annie feels strangely relieved that her devious behaviour hadn't managed to derail the sincere man of God. However, her anxiety increases as she senses that the discussion about her wedding may have brought the review of her life to a close.

Chapter 4

Annie's worst fears are realised as Jesus speaks,

"We've watched enough, now, Annie. You can see that every one of your actions had consequences either for you or for others. Most people only think about earthly consequences or the things they can see, but there is a spiritual battle going on all of the time, and those who aren't for Me are against Me."

"I never really thought about that," Annie admits.

"There are those who hear the Word but it is snatched away by the devil before it can take root, like Dean's father. Then, there are some who receive the Word with joy but only last a little while, they fall away when trouble or problems come because of the Word, like Sophie. There are others who listen to the Word but the cares of the world and the deceitfulness of wealth choke it, making it unfruitful….."

"Like Dean…." Annie finishes.

"Yes, but there are also those who sit on the fence, Annie. These people think that by failing to make a decision about Me, they can live their lives as they please. They put off a sincere search for the truth until it's too late. They assume they will live to old age and they can deal with things then…but some die young and meet Me before they are ready."

"If I had only taken the time to search for the Truth, I can't believe I gambled with my soul like that," Annie is terrified as she knows her punishment awaits. After the examination of her life, she also knows she deserves nothing less. She is full of regret which she knows will last for eternity.

Annie feels desperate as she thinks about her family, friends and neighbours; all those she knew and loved on Earth. She has nothing to lose and decides to make one last request of Jesus who is waiting for her final words. Gathering all the sincerity and fervency she can muster, she falls to her knees in front of Him, "Please can someone go from here to warn them?" she begs.

Jesus replies,

"There was a rich man who was clothed in purple and fine linen and who feasted sumptuously every day. And at his gate was laid a poor man named Lazarus, covered with sores, who desired to be fed with what fell from the rich man's table. Moreover, even the dogs came and licked his sores. The poor man died and was carried by the angels to Abraham's side. The rich man also died and was buried, and in Hades, being in torment, he lifted up his eyes and saw Abraham far off and Lazarus at his side. And he called out, 'Father Abraham, have mercy on me, and send Lazarus to dip the end of his finger in water and cool my tongue, for I am in anguish in this flame.' But Abraham said, 'Child, remember that you in your lifetime received your good things, and Lazarus in like manner bad things; but now he is comforted here, and you are in anguish. And besides all this, between us and you, a great chasm has been fixed, in order that those who would pass from here to you may not be able, and none may cross from there to us.' And he said, 'Then I beg you, father, to send him *to my father's house— for I have five brothers—so that he may warn them, lest they also come into this place of torment.' But Abraham said, 'They have Moses and the Prophets; let them hear them.' And he said, 'No, father Abraham, but if someone goes to them from the dead, they will repent.' He said to him, 'If they do not hear Moses and the Prophets, neither will they be convinced if someone should rise from the dead.'" (Luke 16 vs 19-30 ESV)*

Note to Reader

This is a work of fiction. Timings and events surrounding a possible Judgement Day scenario have been depicted. I am not suggesting that my dramatic reconstruction is what will happen, or attempting to reach beyond the detail given in the Bible. My purpose in writing is to make people stop and think about their own lives, and souls, in the context of the story.

From the Bible, we know that each person will one day die and then face judgement. They will have to give an account of their life to God and everything has already been recorded (although probably not on video tape!) They will then spend eternity in either heaven or hell depending on whether or not their sin has been forgiven. Sin can only be forgiven if someone pays the price for it. The price is death. Jesus is the only One able to deal with our sin because He is the only One who lived a perfect life, and therefore has no sin of His own. Jesus can therefore act as a substitute, and our sinful lives can be exchanged for his perfect life, if we trust that He died for us on the cross. Jesus is a bridge between us in our sin and a holy God. These are the things we can be sure about.

Annie Yale and her family do not exist in reality. However, they are representative of many people living on earth without giving God a second thought.

Our society has collectively turned its back on Christianity deciding that the Bible is a collection of myths and sneering at anyone who dares to suggest otherwise.

Please, stop and think.

What if the Bible is true? What if our sin has separated us from God and one day we will stand in front of Him to give an account of our lives. What if God loves us so much that He has already provided a way of escape by sending His Son Jesus to die on the cross for our sins? What if trusting Jesus is the only way to reach heaven and to avoid eternal punishment in hell?

Annie was unprepared when she met with Jesus. The truth is that any one of us could die at any time, none of us is guaranteed tomorrow. It is too late for Annie but as long as you are still alive, it is not too late for you.

The Bible says, *"If you confess with your mouth that Jesus is Lord and believe in your heart that God raised Him from the dead. You will be saved."* (Romans 10 vs 9 ESV)

Printed in Poland
by Amazon Fulfillment
Poland Sp. z o.o., Wrocław